A THOUSAND MELODIES

*A Book of Poems
by Stacy Hinojos*

OCYD Publishing

A Thousand Melodies copyright © 2024 by Stacy Hinojos. All rights reserved.

No part of this book may be used or reproduced in any manner whatsoever without written permission except in the case of reprints in the context of reviews.

Published by OCYD Publishing
www.thesewords.blog

ISBN: 979-8-9912807-0-9

Thank you for purchasing this copy of, *A Thousand Melodies.*

If you enjoyed this book, please leave a review on Amazon and Goodreads!

-Stacy

*I dedicate this book,
with all my love,
to my family & friends.*

*Where would I be
without you?*

PREFACE

I write because I need to write. On the days I don't write, all those heavy feelings I'm experiencing build and they will drown me under waves of concrete that I can't swim out from. Depression for me is very real, as it is for many of you.

After releasing my first book, These Words, I soon found that a lot of what I've felt and experienced are not felt by me alone. For those of you brave souls who sent me screenshots of your notes and journals, and to those of you who sent me heartfelt messages of your very own experiences, I thank you and I appreciate you.

A Thousand Melodies includes poems I have written over the years of therapeutic journaling. It also includes poems I wrote because I heard a melody in my head that I couldn't sing. Once again, as it was with my first book, these poems lack titles and are written in my own style.

A THOUSAND MELODIES

never knowing
but always feeling...

soul upon soul
heart upon heart
love within love...

never knowing
but always feeling...

looking for a way
to hold you close to me
always...

A THOUSAND MELODIES

strapped into the silence

a void within the dark

full of absence

empty of feeling

quiet next to nothing

searching for something

real

A THOUSAND MELODIES

I won't miss the man
standing in front of me.

But I'll grieve the man
I thought he was.

I long for a place to call home.

A place to heal my heart.

A THOUSAND MELODIES

There is no such thing as being pretty...

There are only different shades of ugly.

A THOUSAND MELODIES

> I want so much more,
> more than I could ever hope for.
>
> There aren't enough days of you.
> I need a forever with you.
>
> A forever that stretches far
> beyond what is earthly.

A THOUSAND MELODIES

Farewell to those I've loved,
for those who remember when.

I have chosen this path,
to leave on my own terms.

Nothing more than a whisper,
something simple, sweet.

Please remember the good times,
of running through the rain.

The times when our laughter
filled the air.

Farewell innocent years,
hidden thoughts and memories.

Farewell to those I've loved.

A THOUSAND MELODIES

Simple words,
Simple phrases,
Bring comfort to me.
They ease my soul.

I weave them,
Into a melody,
That sings to my heart.
And straight into yours.

A THOUSAND MELODIES

I love the mornings after it rains,
when everything smells clean and new.

It makes your eyes open up to a world,
you may have never known or ever seen.

A THOUSAND MELODIES

The belief I had in you
dissolved like sugar
in a warm bath.

You replaced it with
salt and vinegar,
and rubbed it into
old wounds.

Making them live again.
Bringing me to weep again.
Forcing me to grieve again.

A THOUSAND MELODIES

Missing you and all the things you do to me...

Missing the way you make me feel...

Missing the other half of me...

Missing your voice whispering in my ear...

That you love me.

A THOUSAND MELODIES

The list of things I wish I didn't believe about myself,
is over a mile long.

Written in 8-point font,
evenly spaced on beautiful linen paper.

The tiny printing covers
both the front and back.

It is signed with love,
Me.

A THOUSAND MELODIES

Tired of living in a way people expect.

Buried my true self with regret.

Ignoring who I was.

Neglecting my needs.

Now is the time to live for me.

A THOUSAND MELODIES

you are the product of circumstance

it's up to you to embrace what that means

your whole existence cannot be excused

for all eternity

A THOUSAND MELODIES

Words never seem difficult to speak,
when written on a page.

Putting my own voice behind them,
is an entirely different game.

A THOUSAND MELODIES

You're lying there,
so confused,
burning with a fever you never knew.

Searching for light,
in a darkened room,
unaware of the source of the fuel.

A THOUSAND MELODIES

A whisper hint of moon,
floats on the horizon,
fighting its way from behind
the steel black of night.

Clouds waver on high,
shrouding fallen secrets,
as the stars continue
their silent watch.

A THOUSAND MELODIES

She is but an echo

A dream that once was

Floating between

Light and darkness

Madness and joy

A THOUSAND MELODIES

I left my heart
next to your grave

the fresh scent of dirt

in my nostrils
stay

You, and only you
can change.

Heal.
Grow.
Live.

Break the cycles of the past.
Be a trailblazer.

A THOUSAND MELODIES

I'm tired of walking miles
in everyone else's shoes,
when no one will step into mine.

A THOUSAND MELODIES

This space in my heart,
was reserved for you.

It used to be hollow,
and a little frayed.

Like an old newspaper,
caught in the rain.

A THOUSAND MELODIES

Too many words,
absorbed into other ideas.

Never putting in print,
how I truly feel.

Stories left unfinished,
notebooks falling apart.

Another empty pen disposed,
heavy hangs my heart.

A THOUSAND MELODIES

It's impossible to eat when I'm sitting here,
choking back tears.

It's difficult to hold a conversation,
when I can't look you in the eyes.

It's unlikely I'll share my truth with you,
when you only feed me lies.

And my stomach is full.

A THOUSAND MELODIES

What is survival?

Consider the autumn leaves that hold tight
through the brutal days of winter.

They bear the weight of ice and snow,
resilient and determined,
while winds gust and blow.

I see you do the same.

A THOUSAND MELODIES

The sky,
despite the warm glow of sun,
feels internally grey.

Tears no longer remain
inside my now hollow heart.

I sit silently and grieve,
next to a grave
that shouldn't bear your name.

A THOUSAND MELODIES

In these moments when

I can't breathe

I search for your face

even if I know you aren't there.

A THOUSAND MELODIES

somehow you healed
a part of me
that I didn't know
was bruised

maybe I simply forgot
because it
happened so
long ago

A THOUSAND MELODIES

Let the words flow,
like the river to the sea.

Let them move you,
opening your eyes to new things.

Let them transport you to another time,
another place.

Let the words wash over you,
drenching your soul.

A THOUSAND MELODIES

Physically, I was present.
Mentally, I was thousands of miles away.
Spiritually, I was broken and alone.

What was presented to me as love,
was a mythical tale of whimsy,
and in the end, all I got was woe.

A THOUSAND MELODIES

How long does it take
until your lies turn into
something you believe?

A THOUSAND MELODIES

you realized he was your home

when you'd search for him

across every room

just to lock eyes

he'd smile

give you that wink

and your knees

would feel weak

A THOUSAND MELODIES

everything echoed in that night air
the damp clinging to our clothes

I'd rather not know what was out there
lurking in the shadows

while the moon played hide and seek
with the trees

A THOUSAND MELODIES

He reached out to me,
through the veil.

Not alive,
not completely dead.

Every night for years,
he'd visit to tuck me in.

A THOUSAND MELODIES

When I was younger,
And not so wise,
I only wanted to belong.

Now that I'm older,
And a little wiser,
I only long for peace.

Peace of mind.
Peace flooding my heart.
Peace in my soul.

A THOUSAND MELODIES

I glanced down at my hand,
Saw the calluses and rope burns,
And realized I was holding on to you,
Far too tightly.

A THOUSAND MELODIES

laying down on his childhood bed

staring up at the peeling stars above his head

booze swirling in his brain

he hoped he'd be able to get up again

A THOUSAND MELODIES

Maiden inspiration...

Ingenious youthful soul...

Vestal word maker...

Come...

Sing sweet things in my ear...

It's time to spin dreams again.

A THOUSAND MELODIES

You might want to watch your tone
and the words you say.

Words hold power.

But so do I.

For I grow enough poison
in my garden to fill your cup.

A THOUSAND MELODIES

paper thin memories

of heart strings pulled

tears escaping from breaking

her heart beats no more

A THOUSAND MELODIES

I was walking in the woods,
the night had long settled in,
and the air held a silence over me.

The storm I feared was moving in,
winds were starting to howl,
and the pines swayed down to me.

I reached up to let them know,
they were not alone,
and the rain began to drench us.

A THOUSAND MELODIES

I sometimes wonder

When the breezes flow
Through the window

Is it you saying hello?

A THOUSAND MELODIES

I have spent years carving

happiness out of rocks

using only my tears

A THOUSAND MELODIES

It is not my job to fix you,
your journey should not eclipse mine.

I will be with you,
but I cannot be consumed by you.

I will help pull you up,
but I will not allow you to pull me into your abyss.

Breathe life into my
stagnant soul.

My bones are tired
and I feel alone.

A THOUSAND MELODIES

Do you sit there
reading these words
and wonder if they are about you?

They are all about you.

A THOUSAND MELODIES

You look very smug
sitting there in the trees,
holding court with the leaves.

You think I won't tell
about the souls you sold,
or the secrets I hold.

I owe you nothing.

A THOUSAND MELODIES

Light dancing in the sky
Those old northern skies
Watched by eyes for millennia

Aurora Borealis
Sunrise Wind
Torches of the Giants Who Spear Fish

We continue to be dazzled
In awe of your midnight ballet full of
Blues, greens, purples, and pinks

"I love you"

was the easiest

lie I ever told

A THOUSAND MELODIES

Reaching out as far as my mind can carry me,
into the deepest dark of night.

I strain for the quiet in the stillest of air,
where the only company I have are my thoughts.

A place where a hush is a million ideas,
and where my heart can sing a thousand melodies.

A THOUSAND MELODIES

hold a place for me

somewhere in your heart

a place safe and warm

where you reach out to me

once in awhile

and think of me fondly

A THOUSAND MELODIES

I have met myself.

And I don't love her.

A THOUSAND MELODIES

Wise beyond his years
grown so fast
he wasn't a little boy
too young to be a man.

With owl's wings
he took to the night sky
no longer in pain
and healed.

A THOUSAND MELODIES

I know that at some point

The book you are holding

Is going to end up on a dusty table

In your front yard or garage

Proudly wearing a cheery yellow

Twenty-five cent sticker

I fear…silence.

Silence between us
that's uncomfortable.

A silence filled with
things left unsaid.

And feelings…unfelt.

A THOUSAND MELODIES

the Earth needed this rain

my soul craved it as well

it has been thirsty and

needed to be cleansed

A THOUSAND MELODIES

I remember everything you said.

Although, I said I didn't understand.

You said I dulled your light.

So, I decided to go away.

And you wonder why I didn't stay.

Depression…

Sleep without dreaming.

Eating without tasting.

Waking without purpose.

Breathing…

Calling
Calling for you
Through the mist
The forest blue
And dust of moons

A THOUSAND MELODIES

The moon has a song of her own,
that she sings as the night grows short.

It's quiet and soft,
melodic as a lullaby.

We hum it during the day,
not remembering the words.

A THOUSAND MELODIES

> Poets write
> because we
> cannot sing
> the melodies
> we hear in
> our hearts.

A THOUSAND MELODIES

While everyone held their breath,
Waiting for the hero to fall,
I was waiting for him to fly.

A THOUSAND MELODIES

I'm nostalgic for something
A deep love
A soul connection

Anything that leaves my body
Feeling like a limp noodle
Forgotten in the bottom of a pan

A THOUSAND MELODIES

I didn't suddenly become selfish.
I started saying, "no".

I put myself first.
I chose to place boundaries.
I stopped listening to your lies.
I no longer wanted to be hurt by your words.

I decided to live my life for me.
And regrets are few.

A THOUSAND MELODIES

I like the dark.

I can't see my reflection there.

No one can see my scars.

If I'm silent, I can cry undisturbed.

And when I hold my breath, it's like I'm not there.

A THOUSAND MELODIES

Sad
Beautiful
Brokenness.

How you embrace me
As tightly as anything can.

A THOUSAND MELODIES

I lulled myself into a false sense of security.

It was easier to ignore what was happening,
than to face it.

In the end, I knew I would be hurt.

A THOUSAND MELODIES

Most nights she falls asleep

Easily within reach

And slumbers

To the sounds of pen

Scratching on paper

A THOUSAND MELODIES

There are so many people to cry for,
But half of them don't deserve my tears.

A THOUSAND MELODIES

I don't feel anything.

Of course
you don't,
you're dead.

A THOUSAND MELODIES

what can I do
my heart belongs to you
you leave me so blue
every time you leave the room
what else can I do

A THOUSAND MELODIES

There is an empty spot in my heart,
And I don't remember what lived there before.

Maybe it's the love I once had for myself,
Before the world told me I wasn't enough.

A THOUSAND MELODIES

She finally felt it,
or the lack of it.

The heaviness had lifted
and she felt lighter.

Lighter than she had been in years,
both mentally and physically.

A THOUSAND MELODIES

I wonder if she remembers giving me
the pretty leather journal for my birthday.

I wonder if she realizes that I filled every page,
each line with memories of her.

I wonder if she would know
that the first half was filled with joy,
and that the rest was filled with pain.

A THOUSAND MELODIES

Hold me until the sun meets the sky,
and the birds begin to sing.

Slay the demons that haunt me,
so I can close my eyes to sleep.

ACKNOWLEDGEMENTS

Books do not happen overnight, nor do they happen without love, support, encouragement, and a huge dose of reality.

Scott Hinojos, thank you for reading this book so often, especially those first rough drafts, and offering some exceptionally clever ideas, beginning to end. **Henry**, thank you for being proud of me, and not complaining about having to eat cereal so often. I love you both! **Kelli Cornelius**, thank you for pulling me out of my negative headspace when I need it, and putting the finishing touches on the editing process. I couldn't have finished this book without you. **JoAnna Vaillancourt Burditt**, thank you for all our conversations, not only concerning this book, but everything else. I look forward to collaborating with you on my next book! To **John Harper**, **Erin Newby**, and **Sharon & Ron Klemm**, I love you!

Thank you to everyone on social media for not only sharing my blog, but my posts and videos. Your continued support and encouragement are greatly appreciated. To the folks who have taken part in all the meditation sessions, thank you for all your wisdom, and allowing me the space to simply be me. To all my family and friends, thank you for your love and support, while offering me some beautiful feedback. I appreciate how we were able to connect over *These Words*, which truly ended up being *Our Words*.

Finally, to those of you who are struggling in life, for whatever reason, you are important. You matter in ways you might not be able to recognize, but you do. I'm proud of you for making it another day, and I'll see you tomorrow.

About the Author

Stacy Hinojos (ee-no-hos) was ecstatic to publish her first book of poetry, *These Words*, in March 2024.

"I've been writing since I was 12, but poetry has always been my favorite medium." Stacy writes from the heart, raw and unapologetic, using writing as a form of therapy.

Stacy was raised along the shores of Chequamegon Bay area, surrounded by many mentors. She lives in Wisconsin Rapids with her husband Scott, and their son Henry. *A Thousand Melodies* is her second book.

Find more about Stacy
www.thesewords.blog

OTHER WORKS BY STACY HINOJOS

These Words

Available on Amazon

www.ingramcontent.com/pod-product-compliance
Lightning Source LLC
Chambersburg PA
CBHW061339040426
42444CB00011B/2990